BEAVER BOOKS

My First Bilingual Book · Mon premier livre bilingue

Colours

Les couleurs

English-French · Français-anglais

— **A child's first book of words and fun – in two languages!** —
— **Un livre bilingue, rempli de mots et de plaisir pour les tout-petits!** —

red

bleu

yellow

jaune

green

vert

orange

orange

purple

violet

pink

rose

brown

brun

grey

gris

black

noir

white

blanc

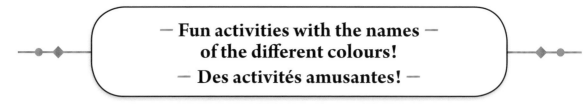

— Fun activities with the names — of the different colours!
— Des activités amusantes! —

Can you say the names of these colours, in both French and English?
Nomme en français et en anglais toutes les couleurs qui sont présentées ici.

Say each colour word and find its picture in the book.
Prononce les mots que tu vois ici et retrouve les couleurs correspondantes dans le livre.

| **white** | **brown** | **green** | **red** |
| **blanc** | **brun** | **vert** | **rouge** |